AMERICAN MUSCLE CARS

COLORING BOOK

GOLDEN BOX

This book belong to

COLOR TEST

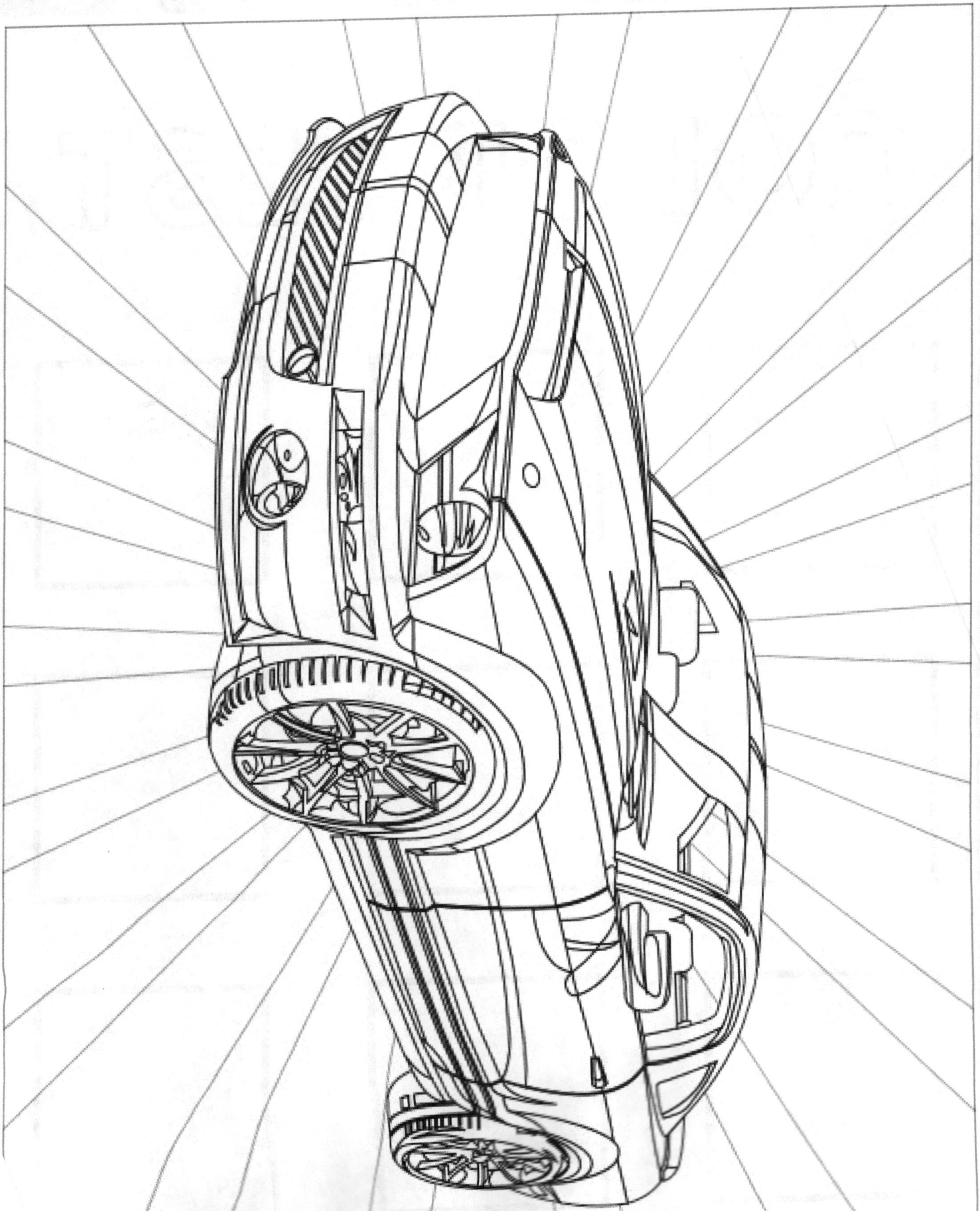

COLOR TEST

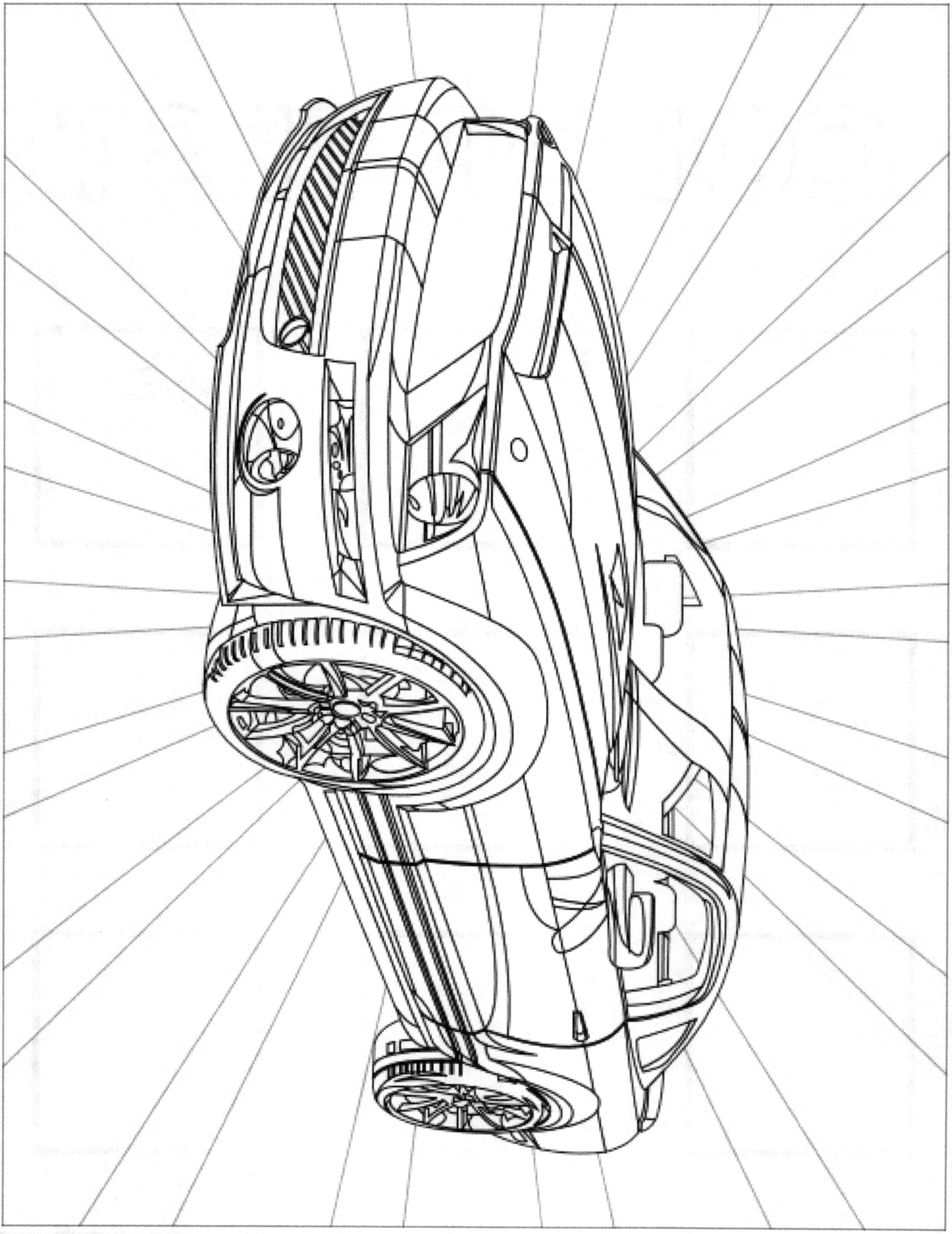

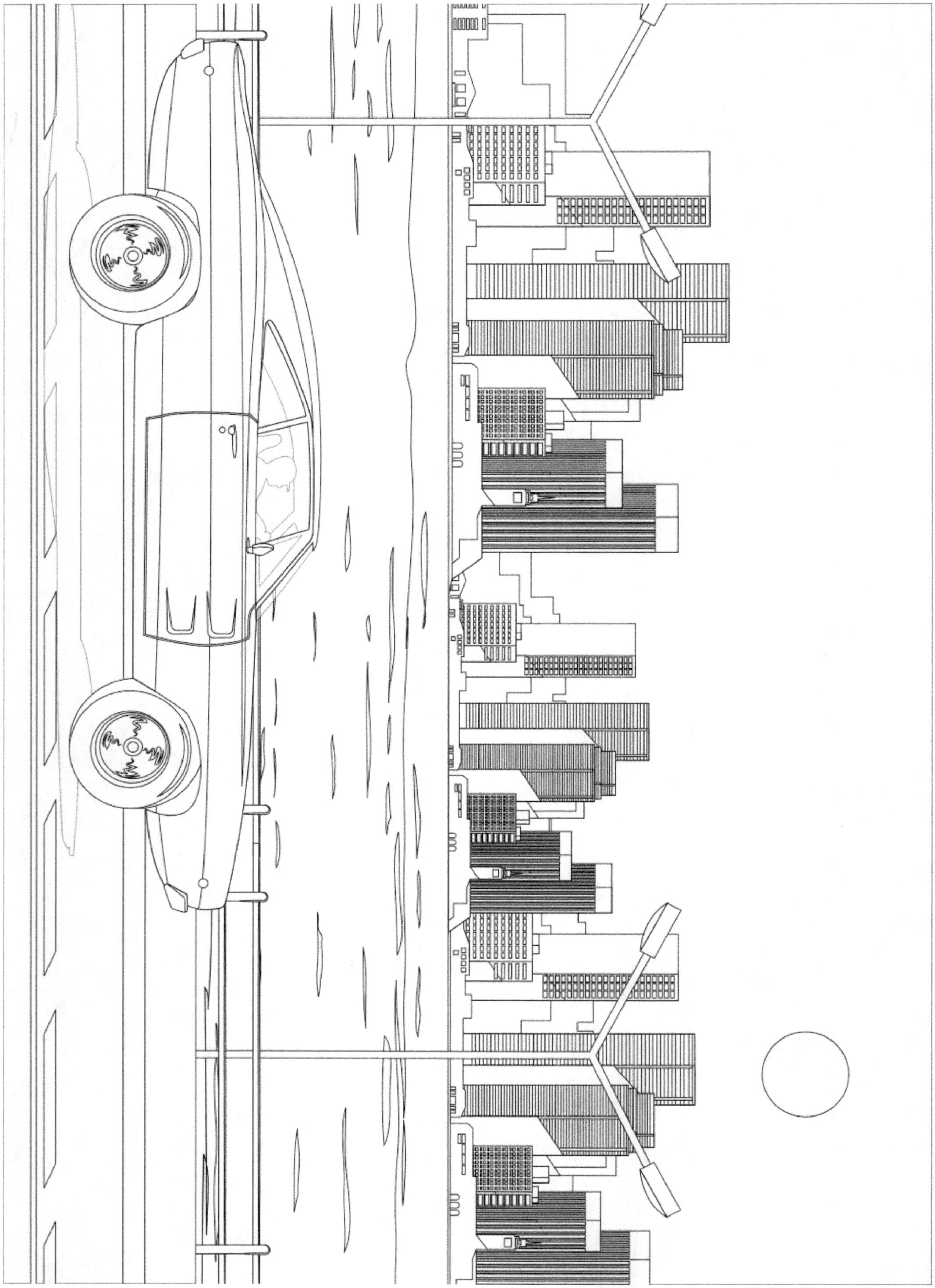

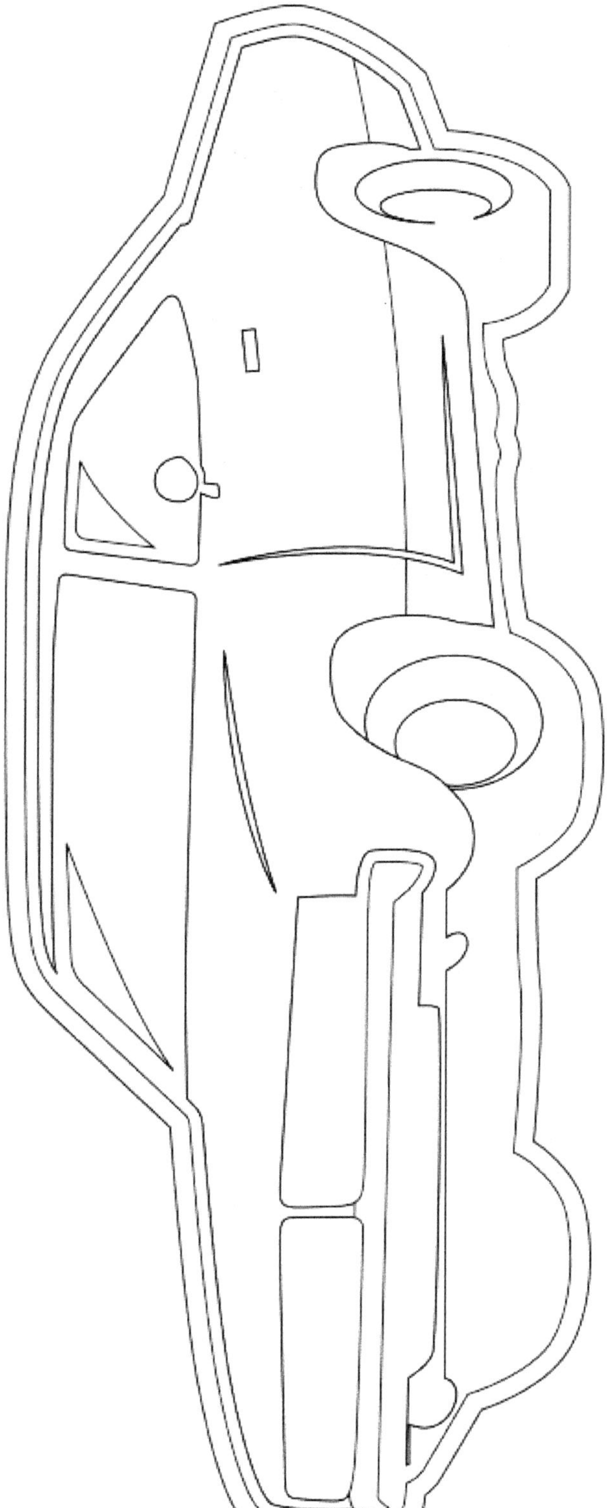

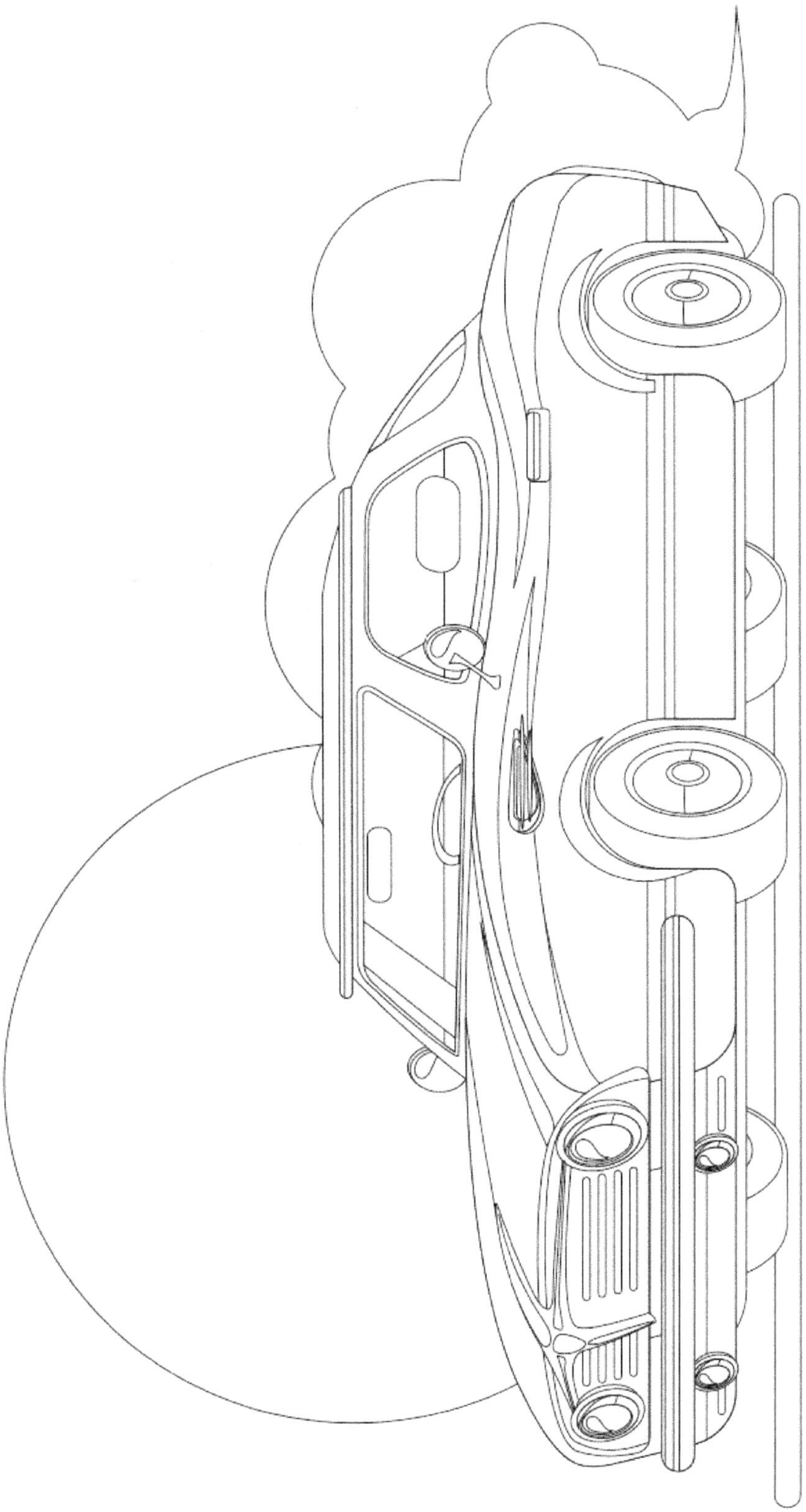

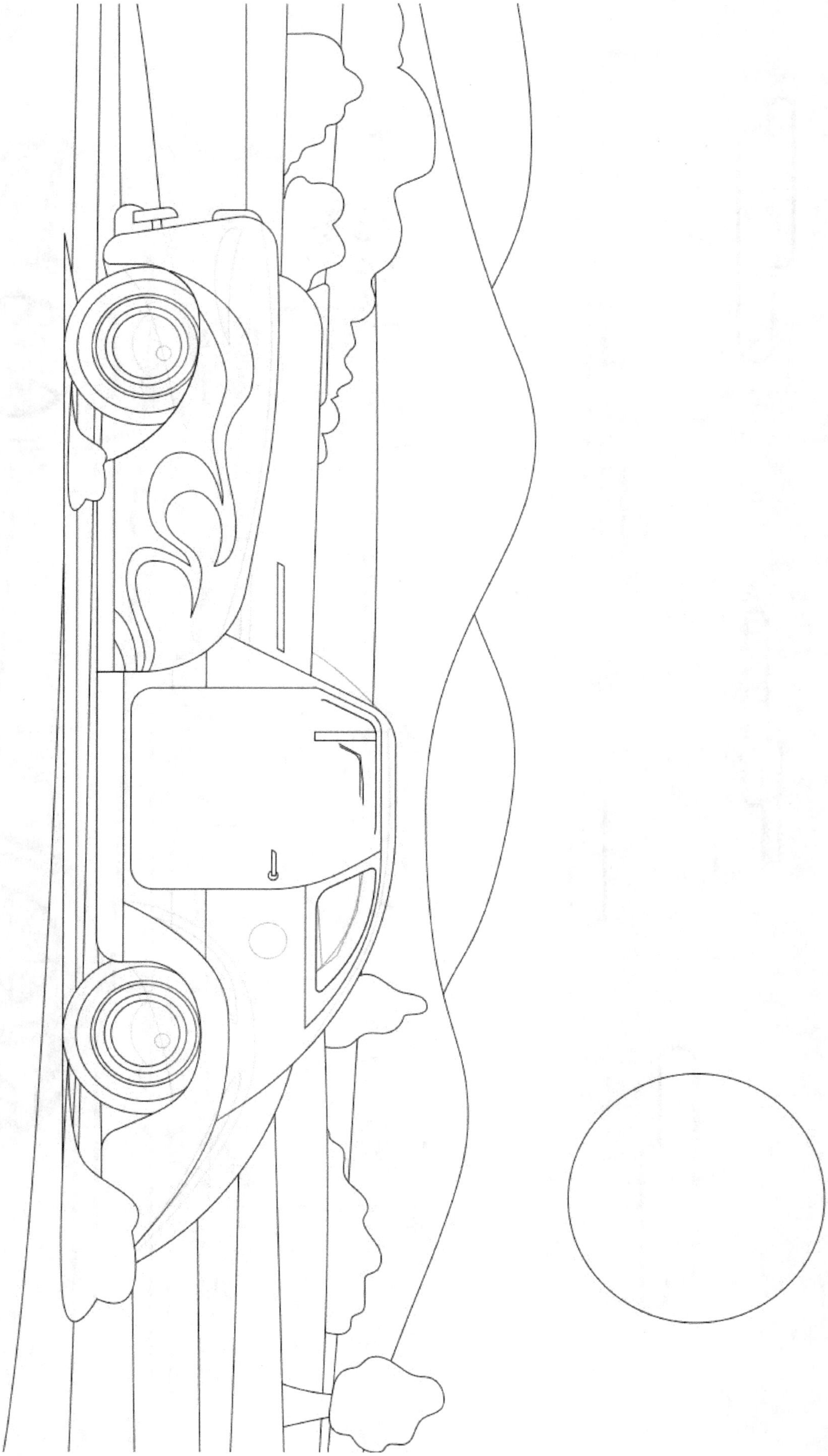

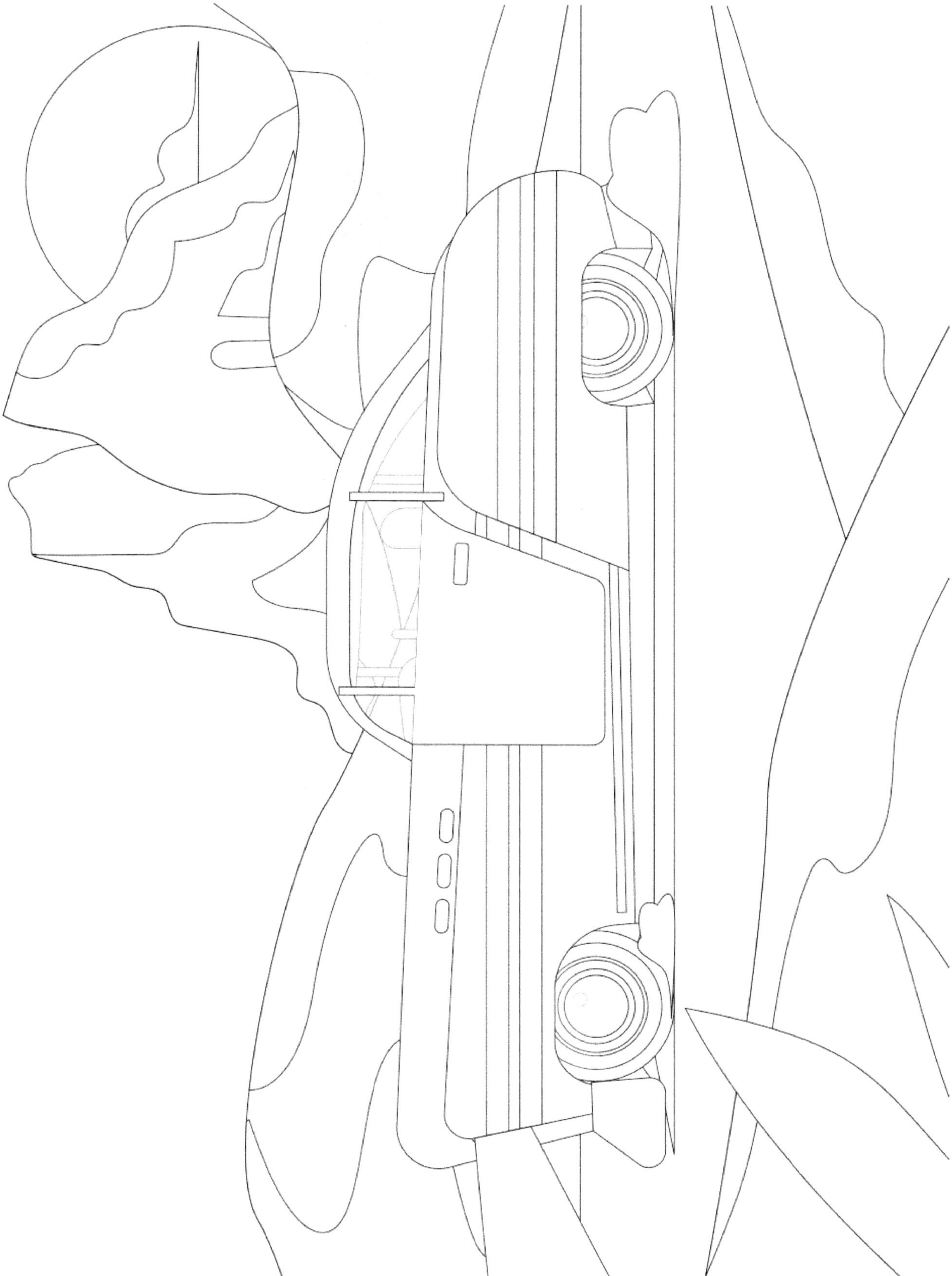

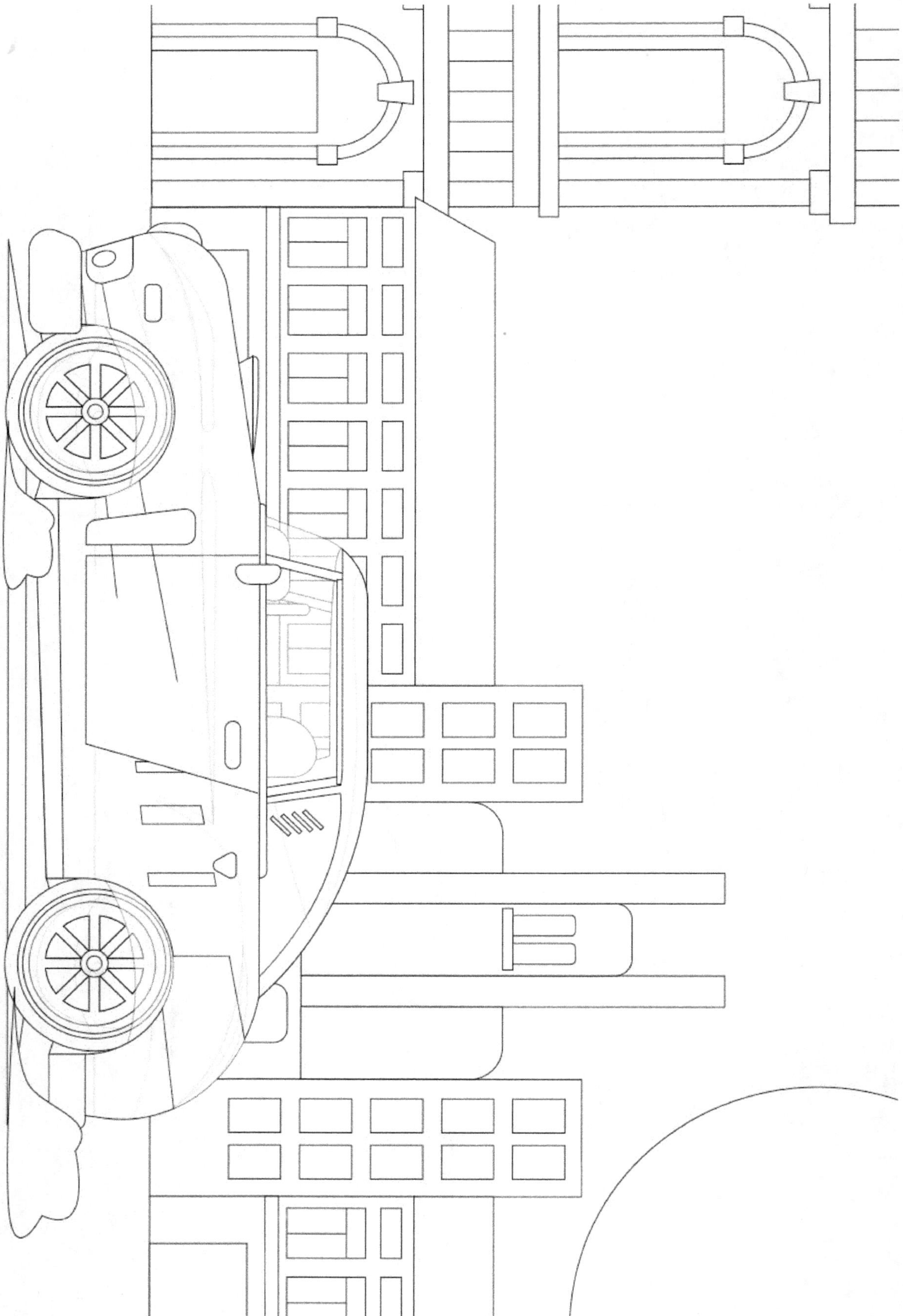

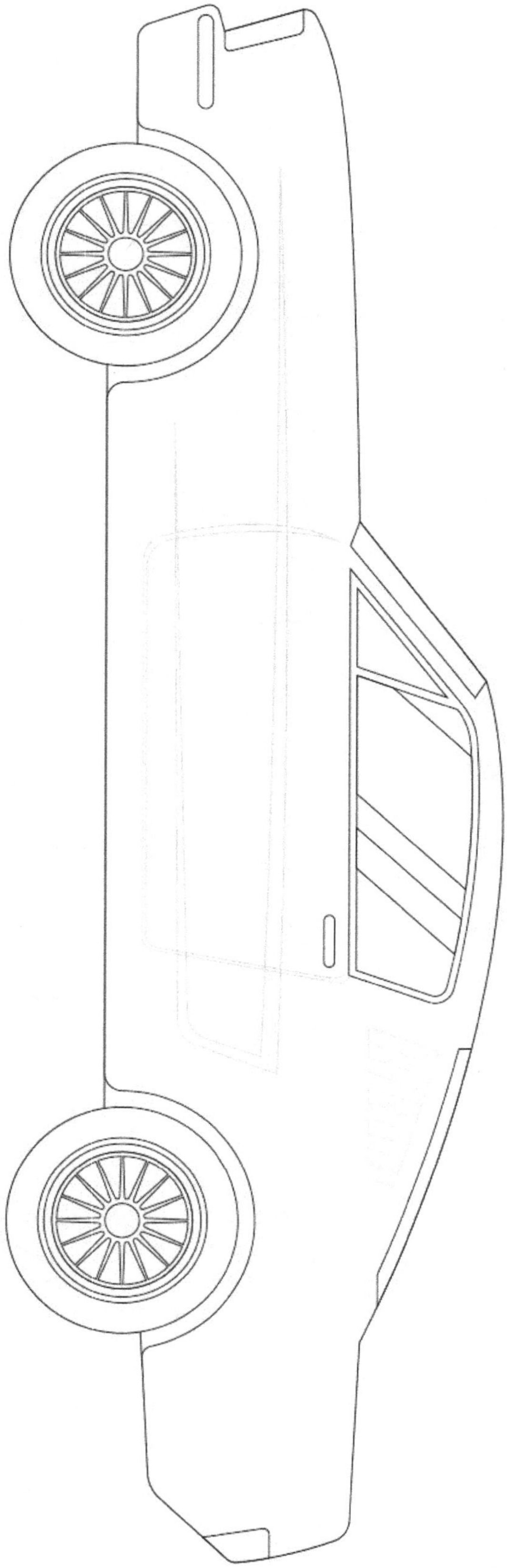

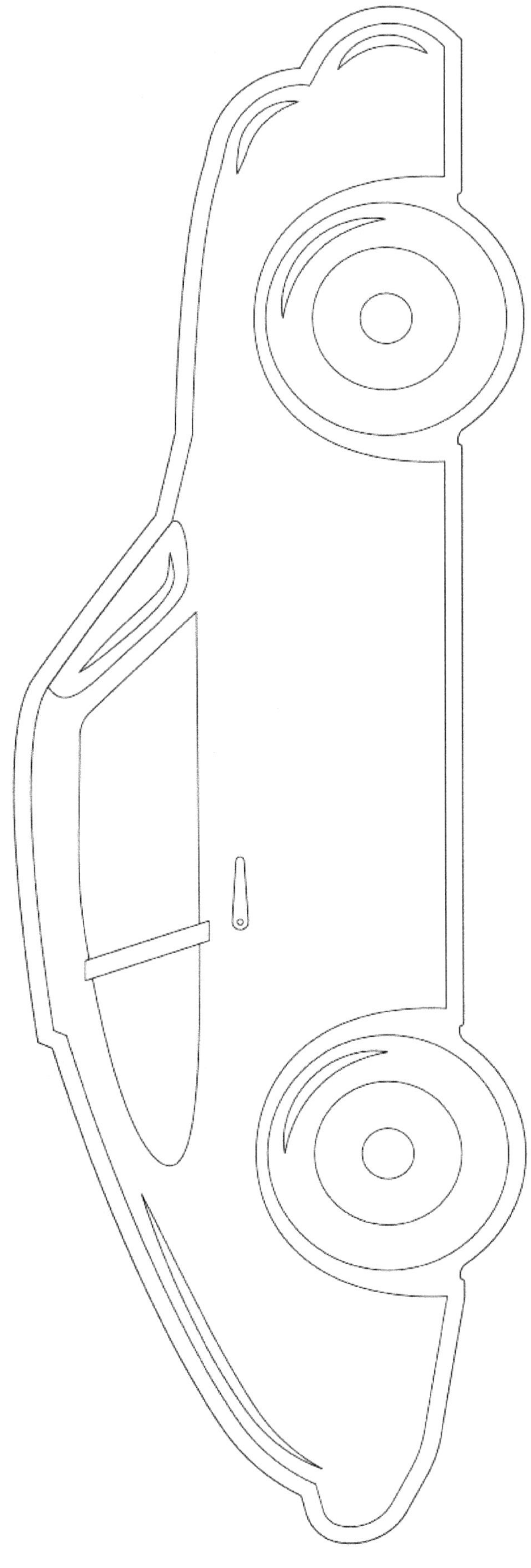

BURNOUT

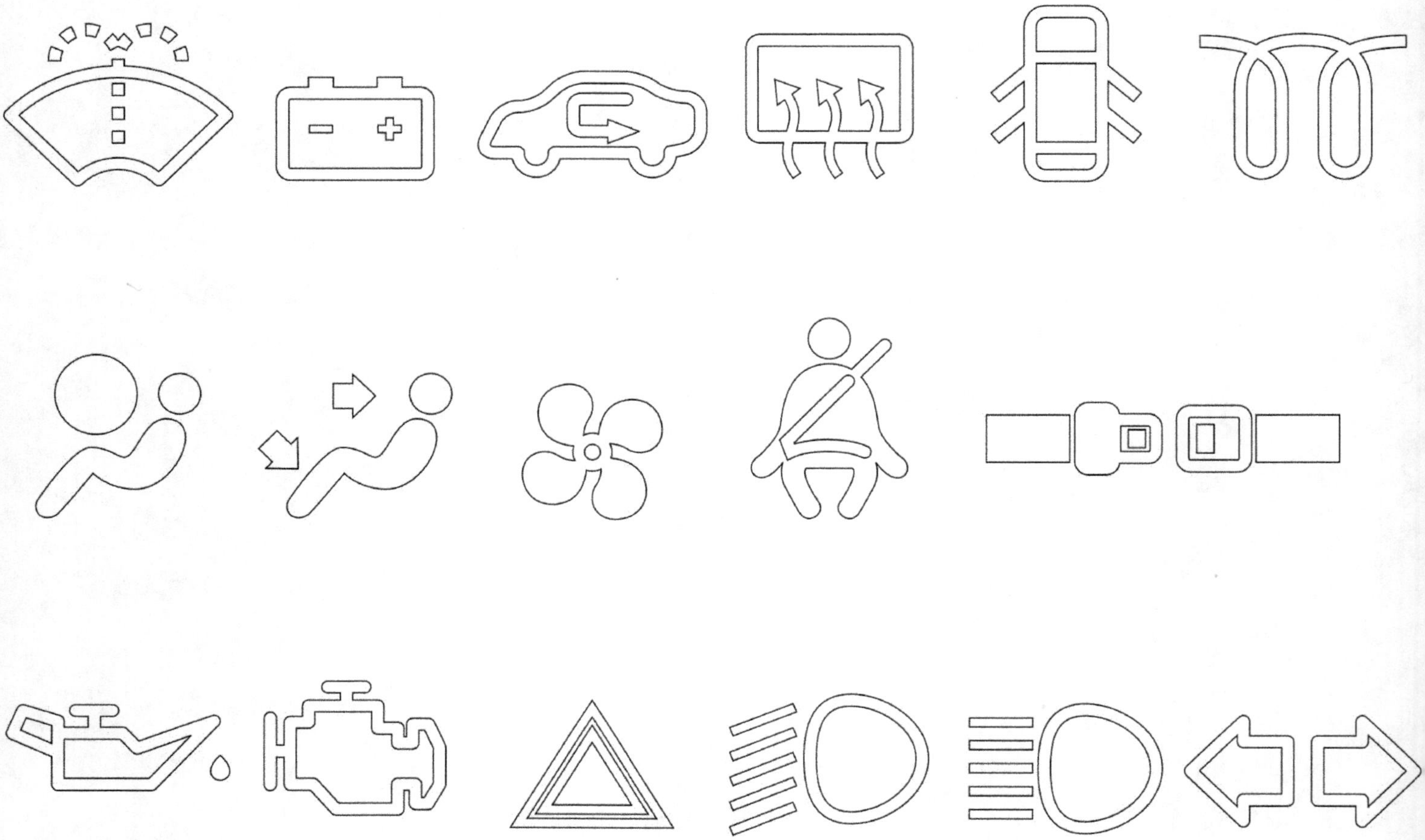

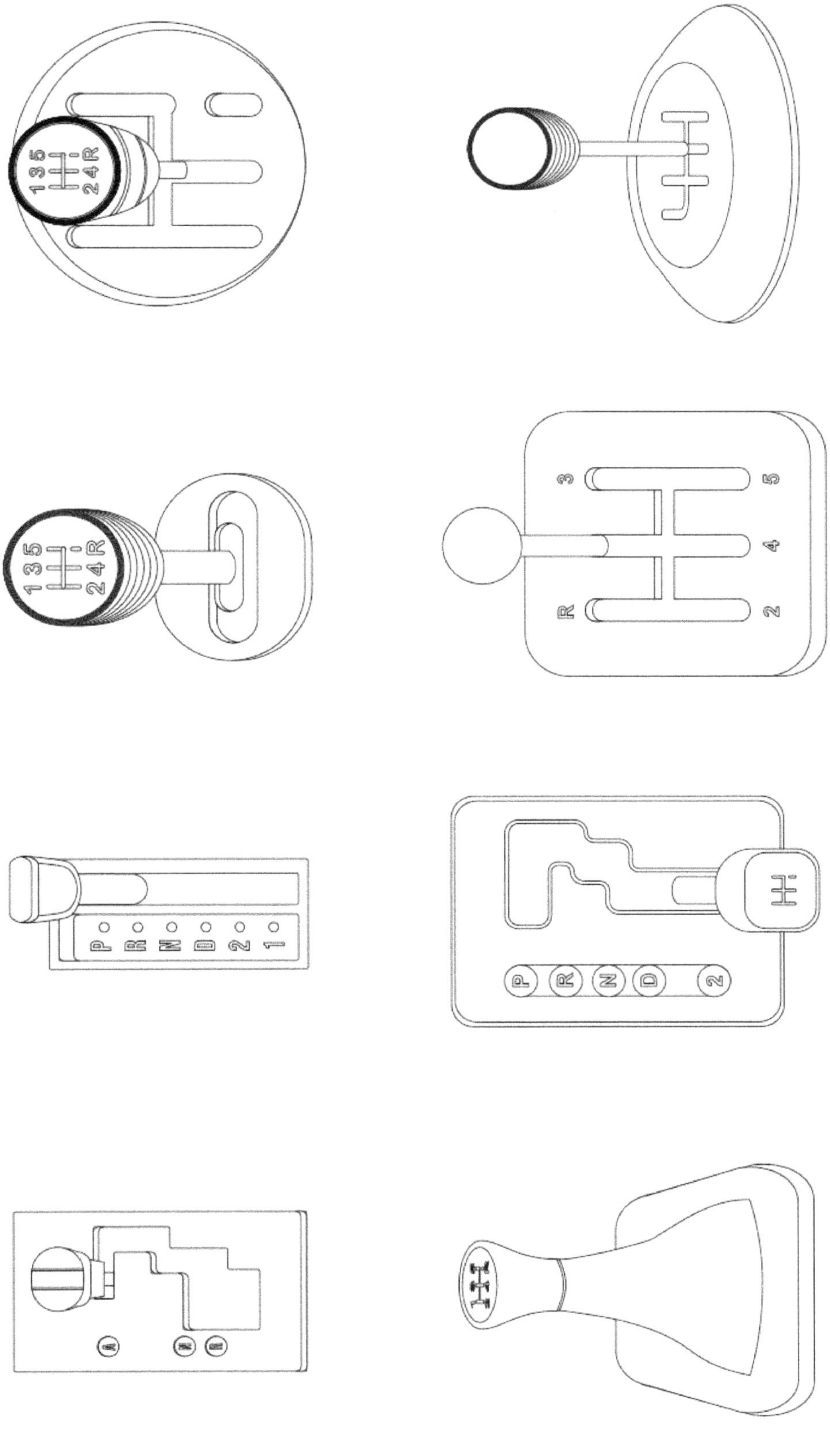

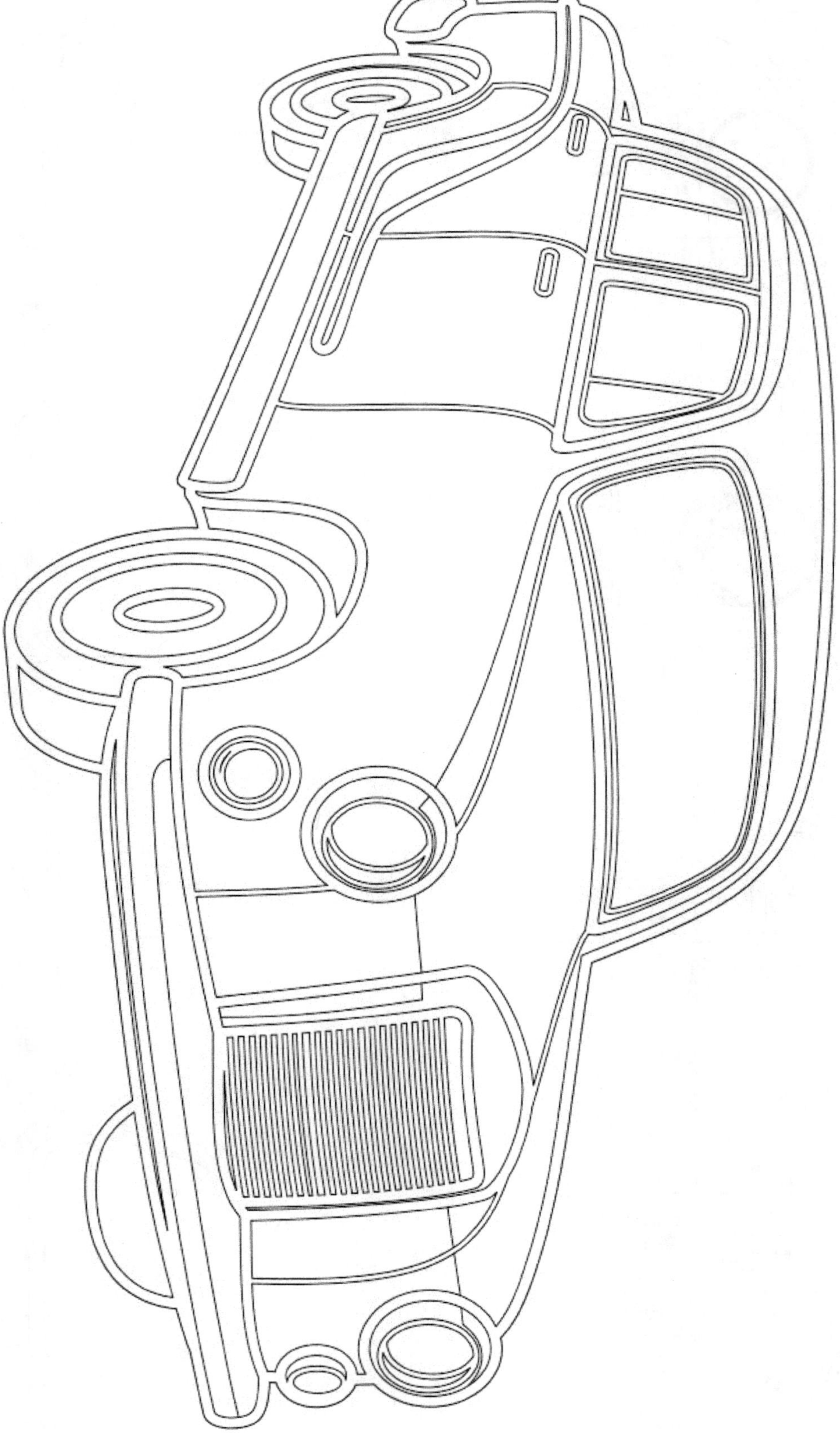

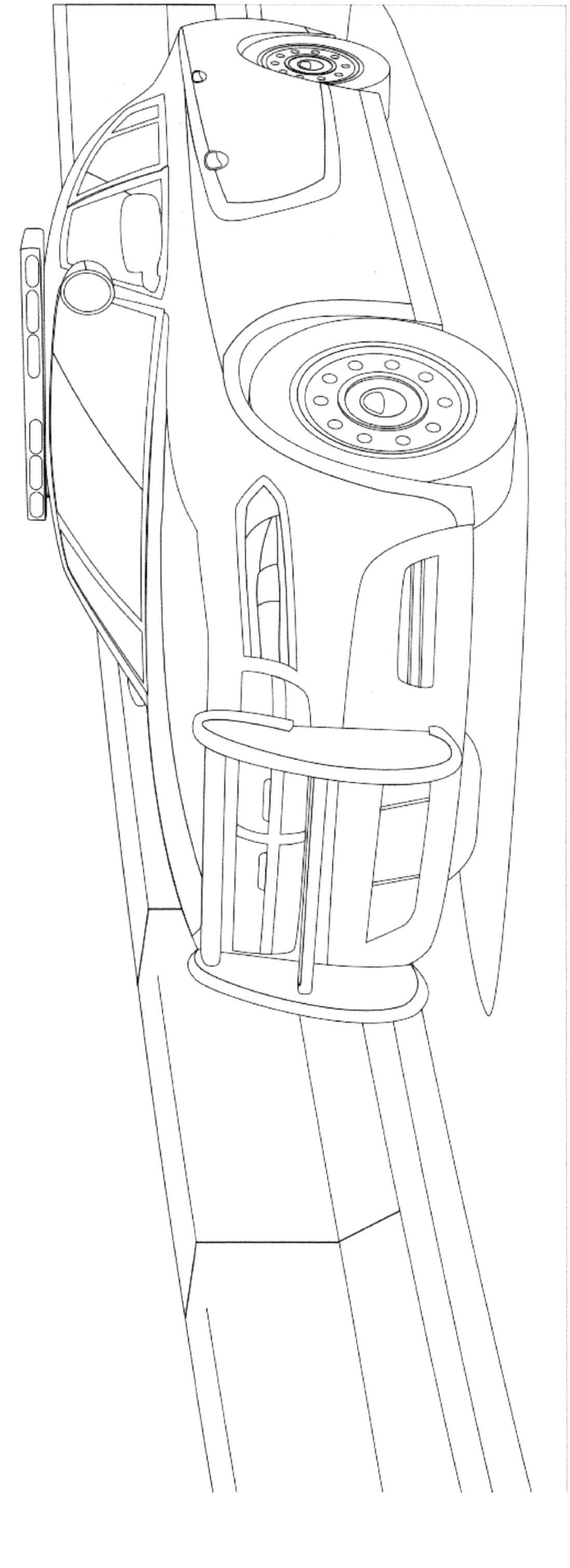

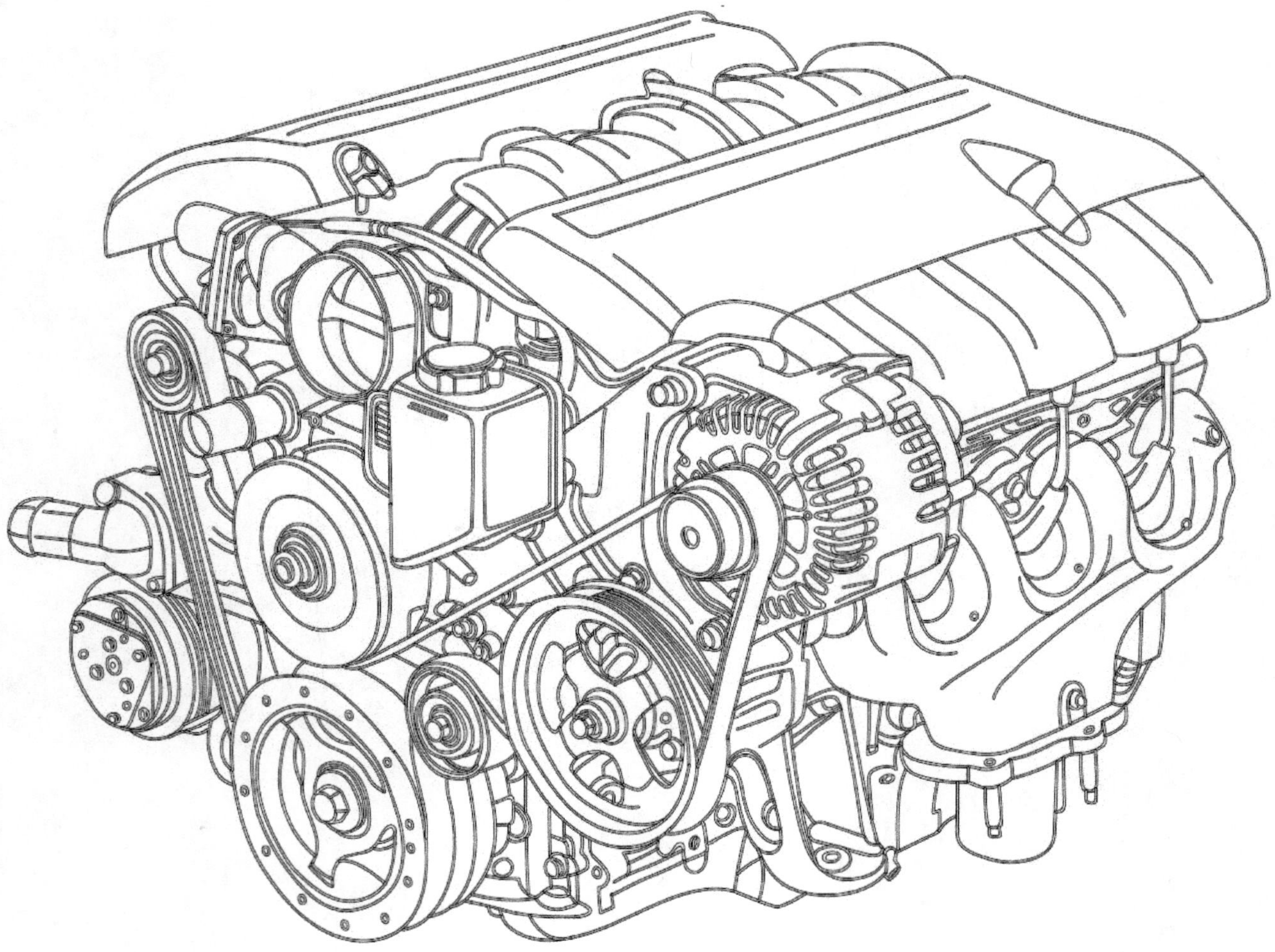

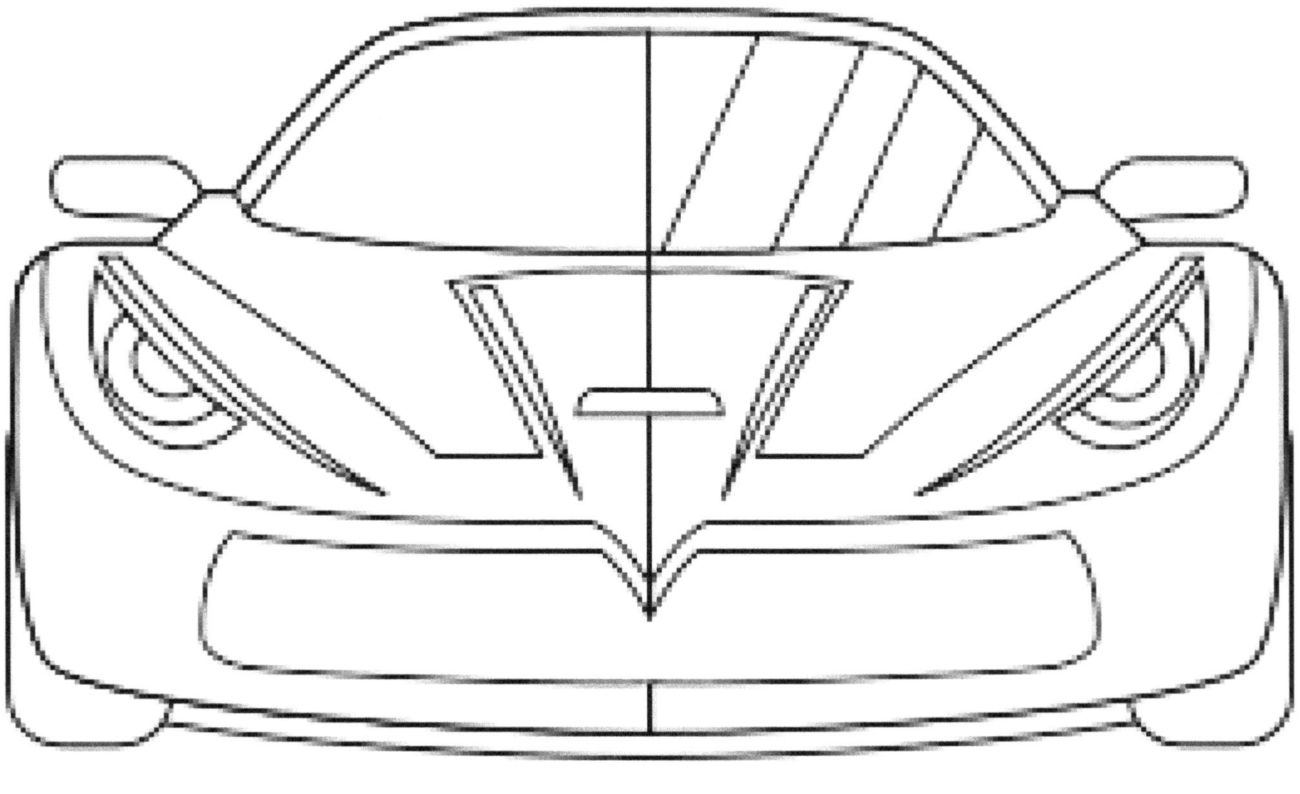

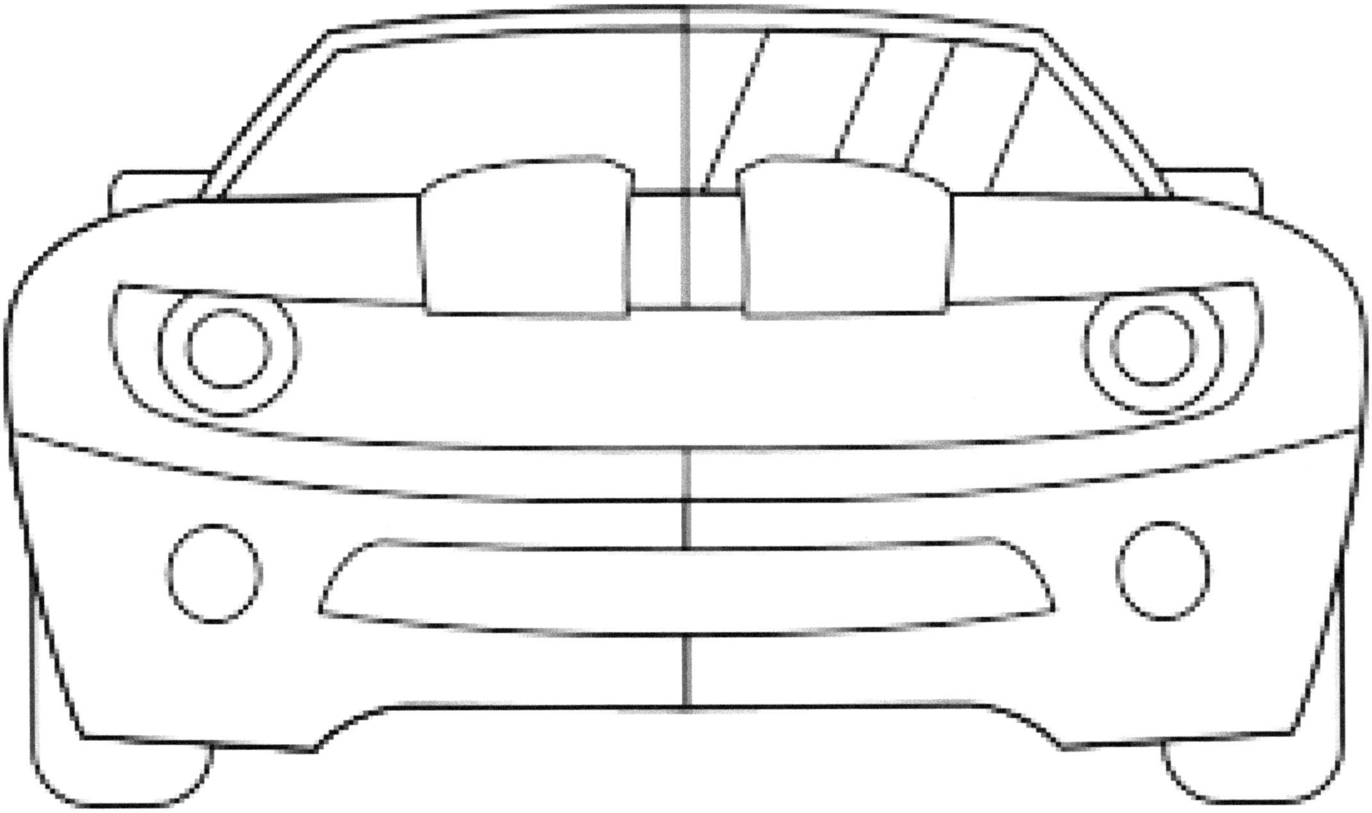

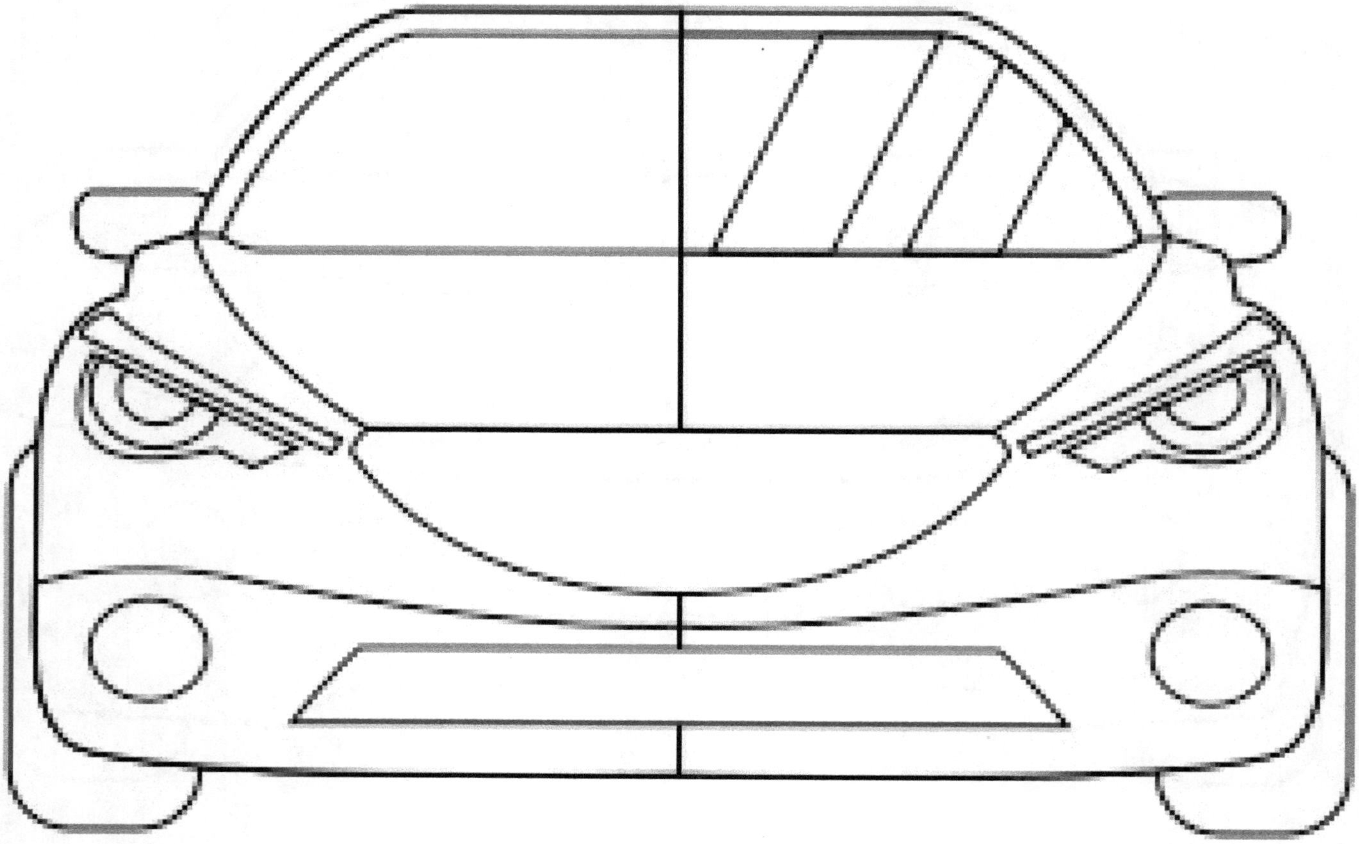

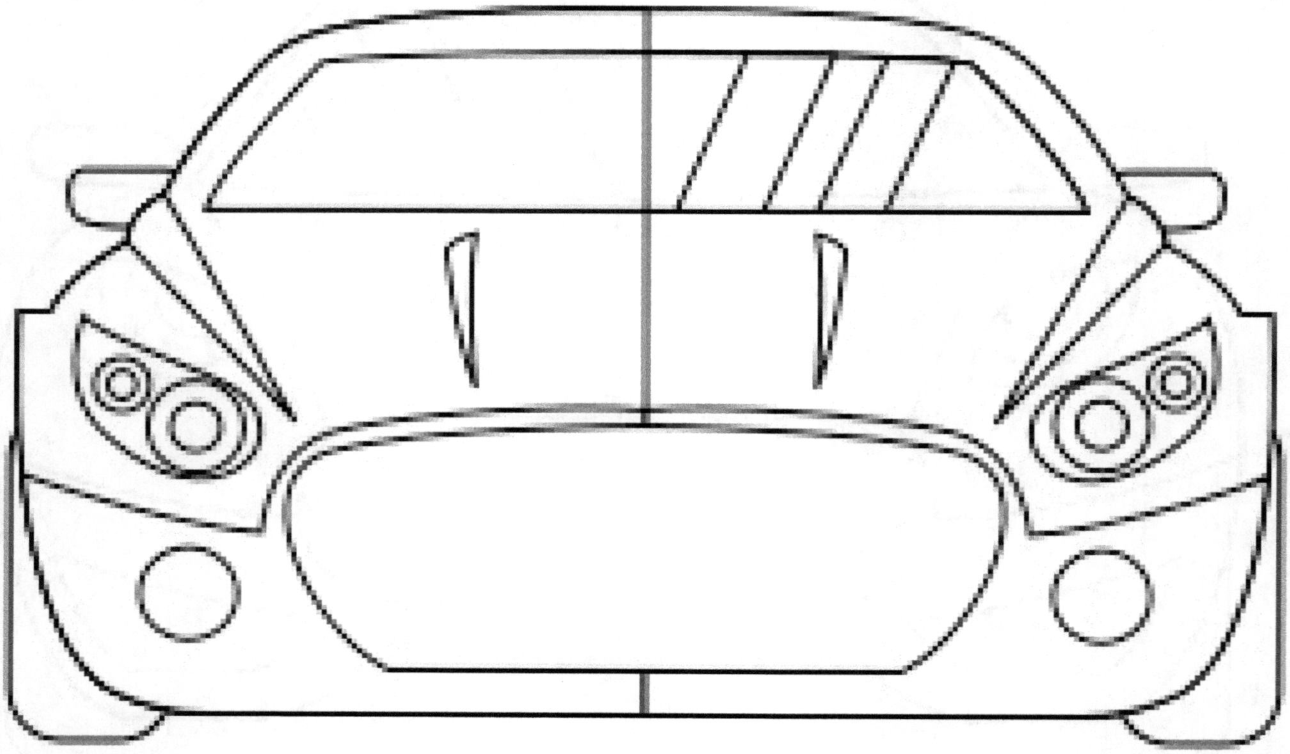

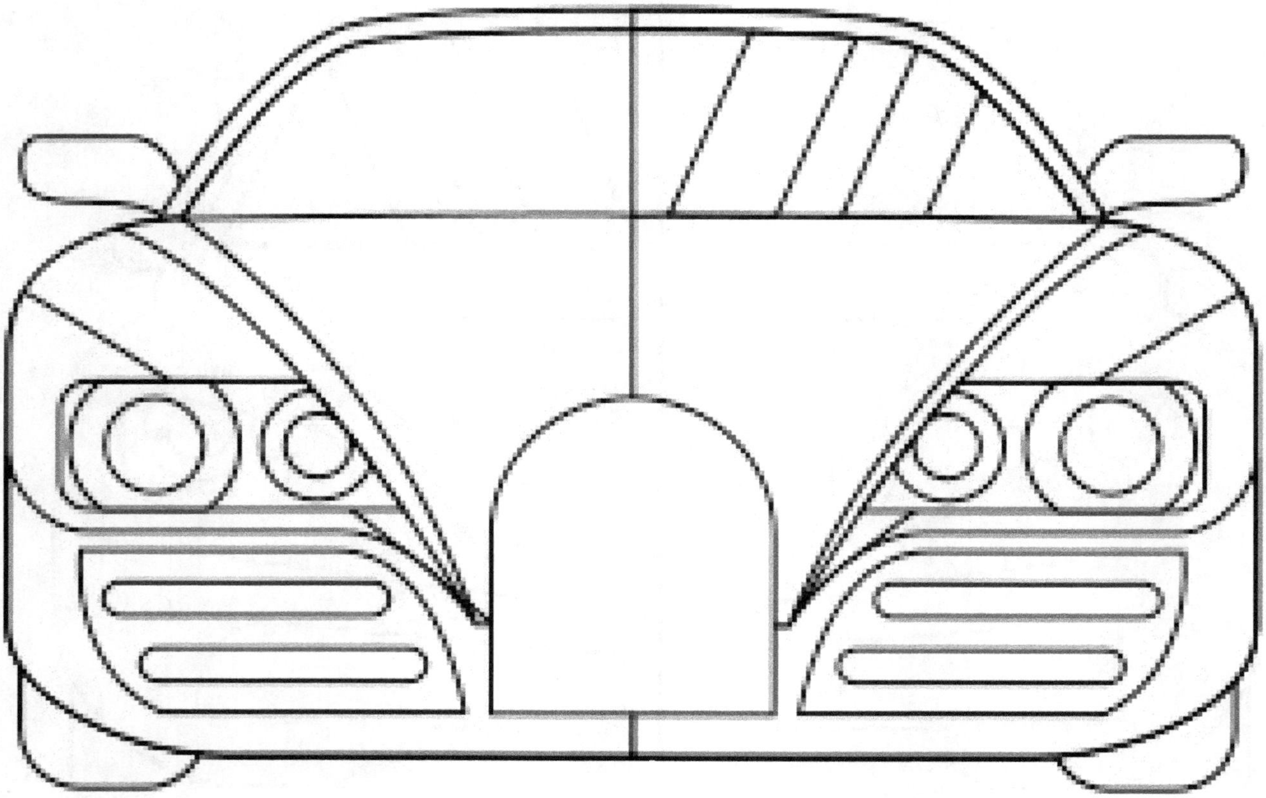

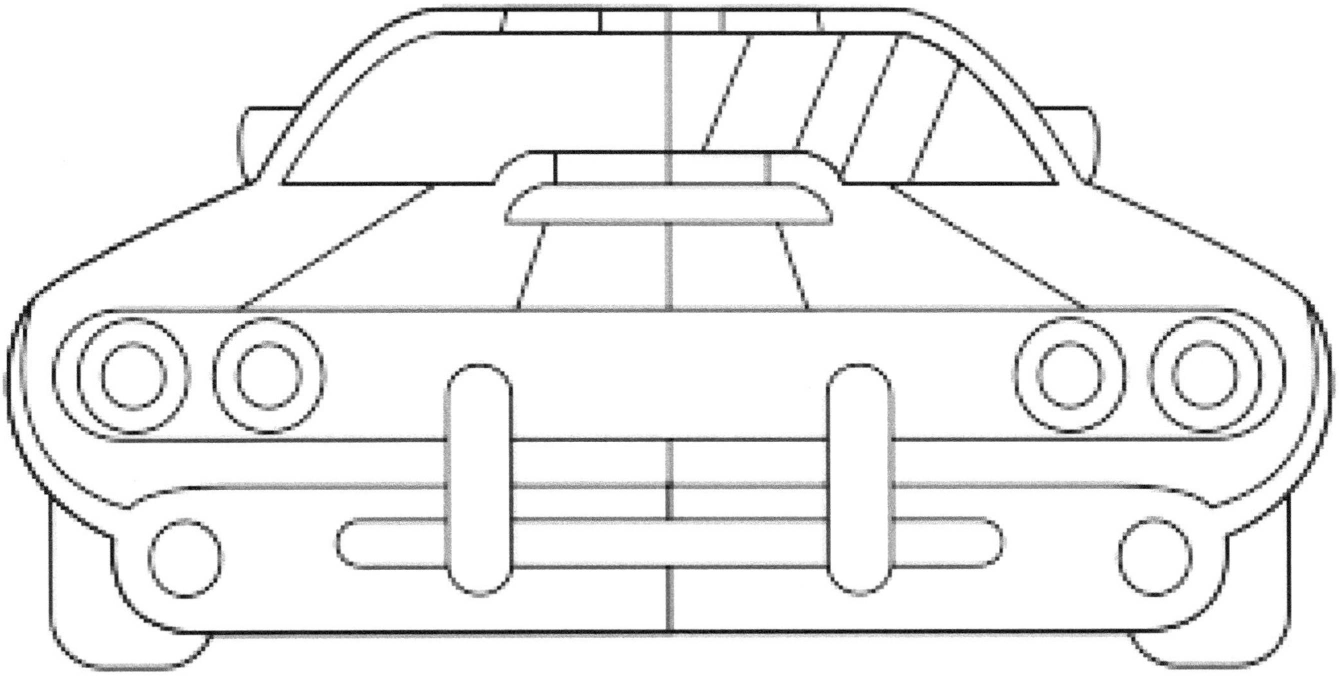

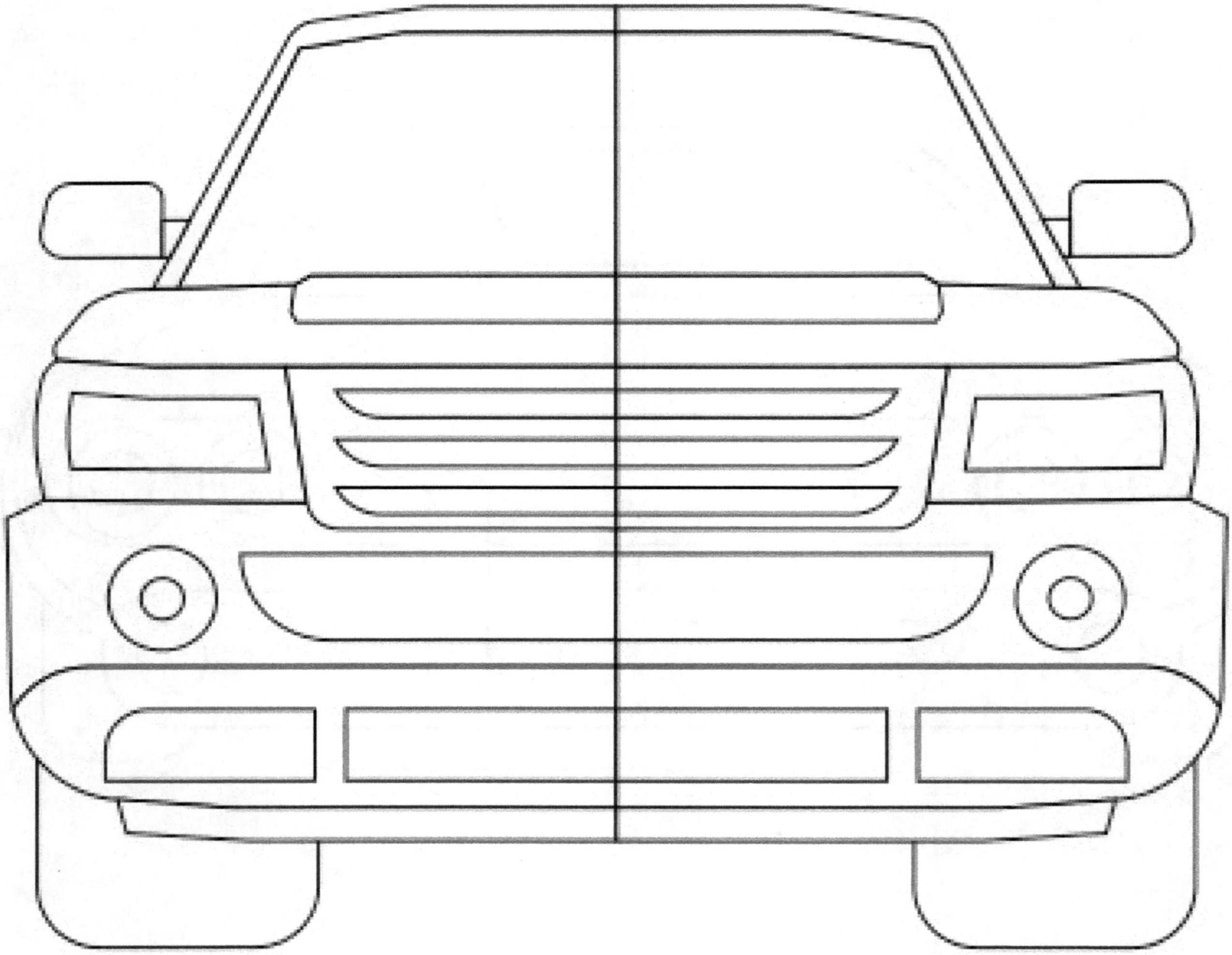

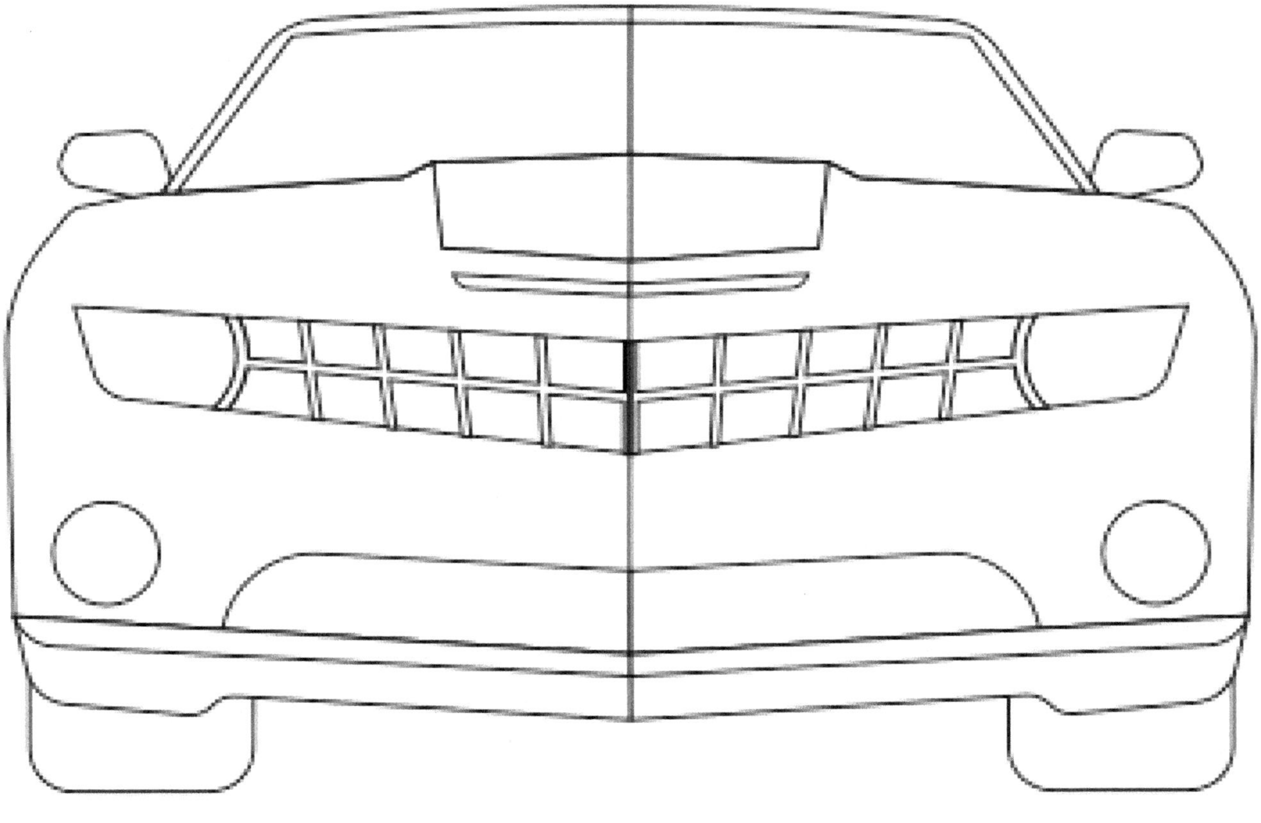

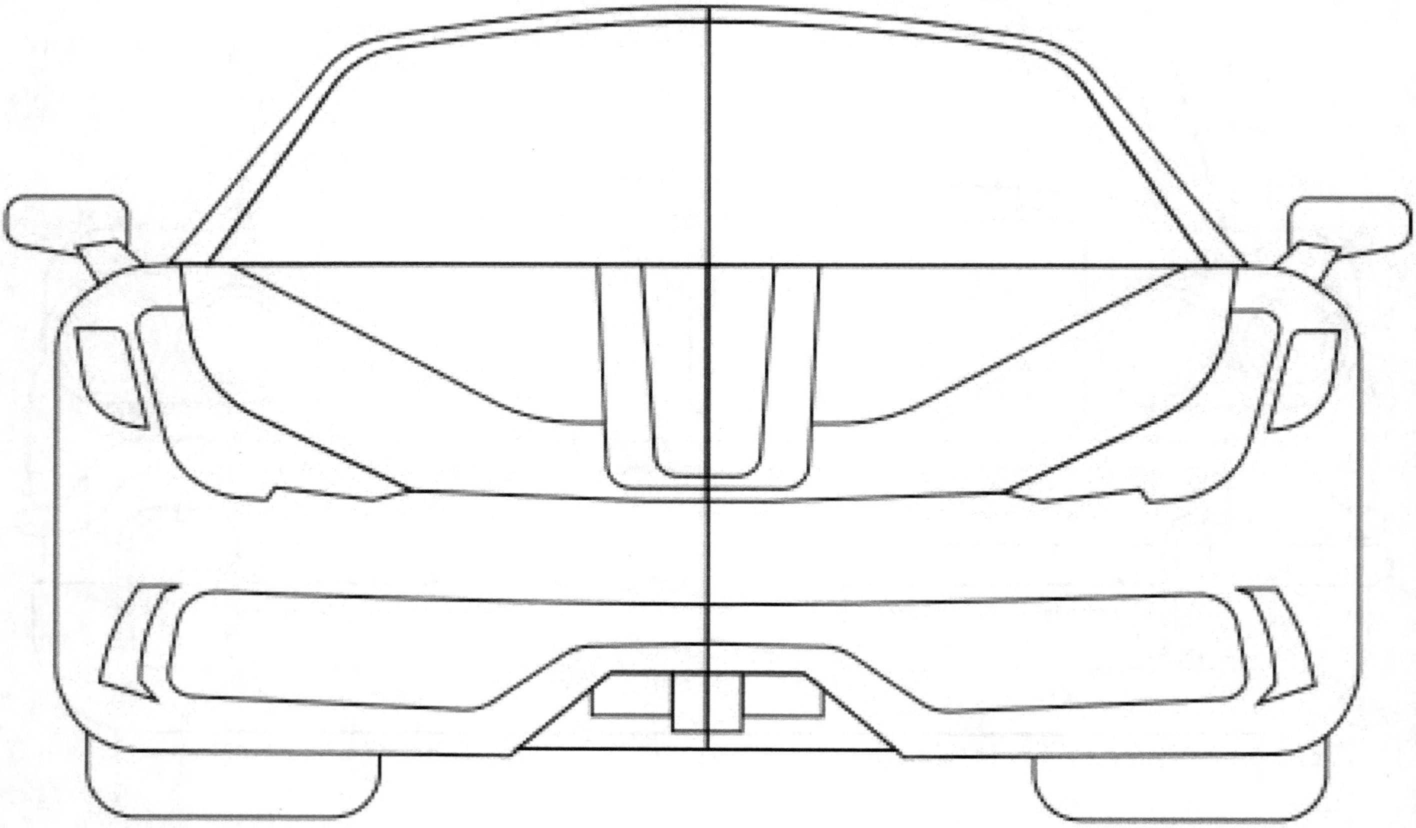

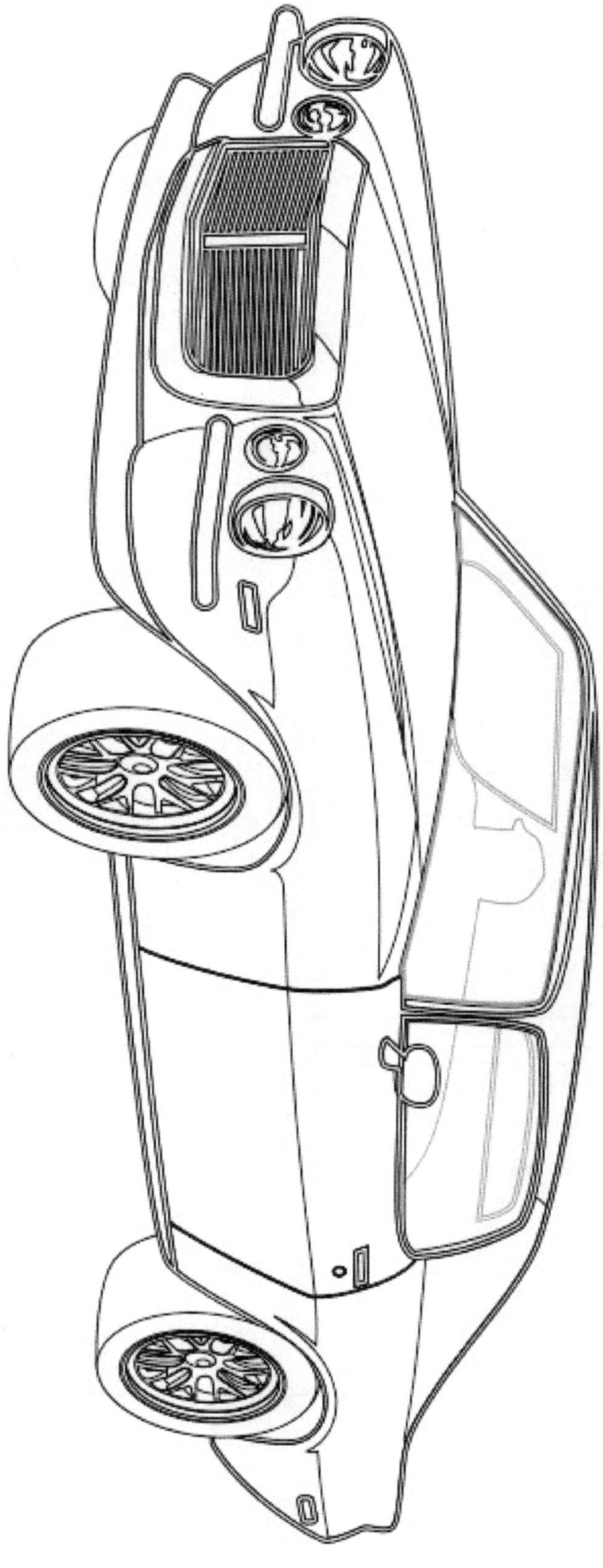

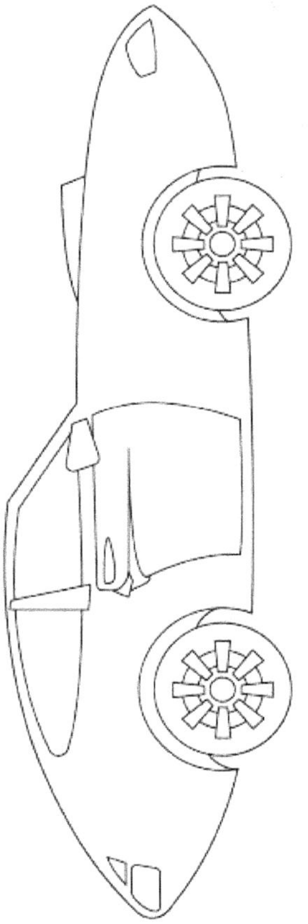

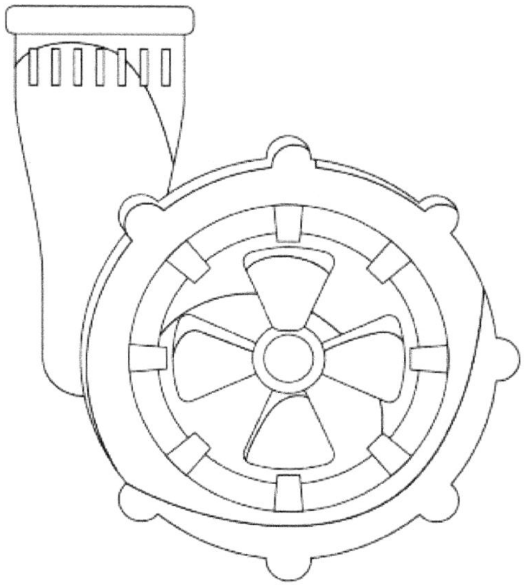

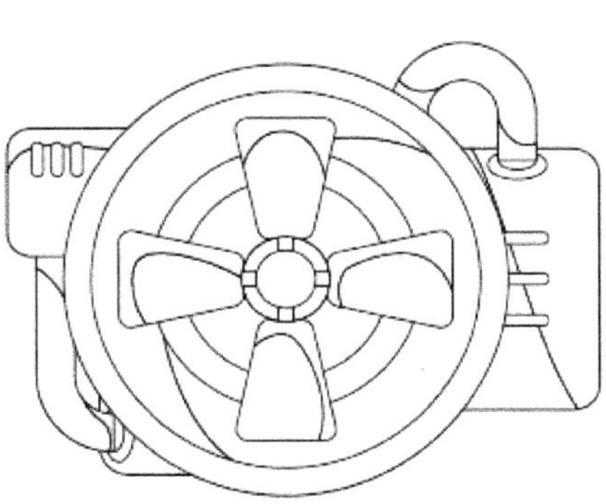

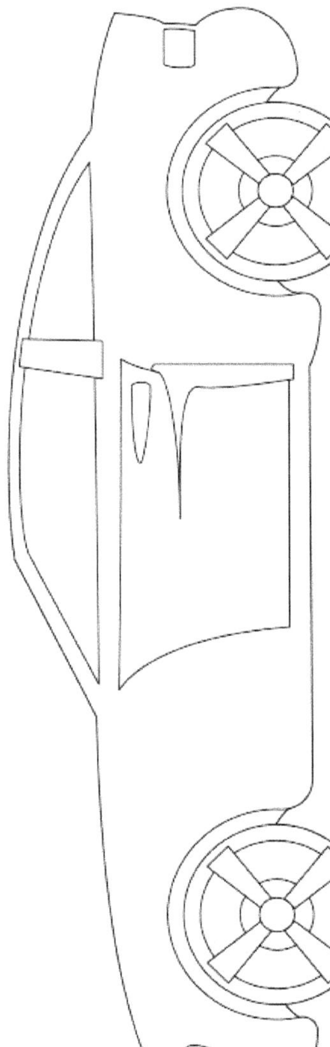

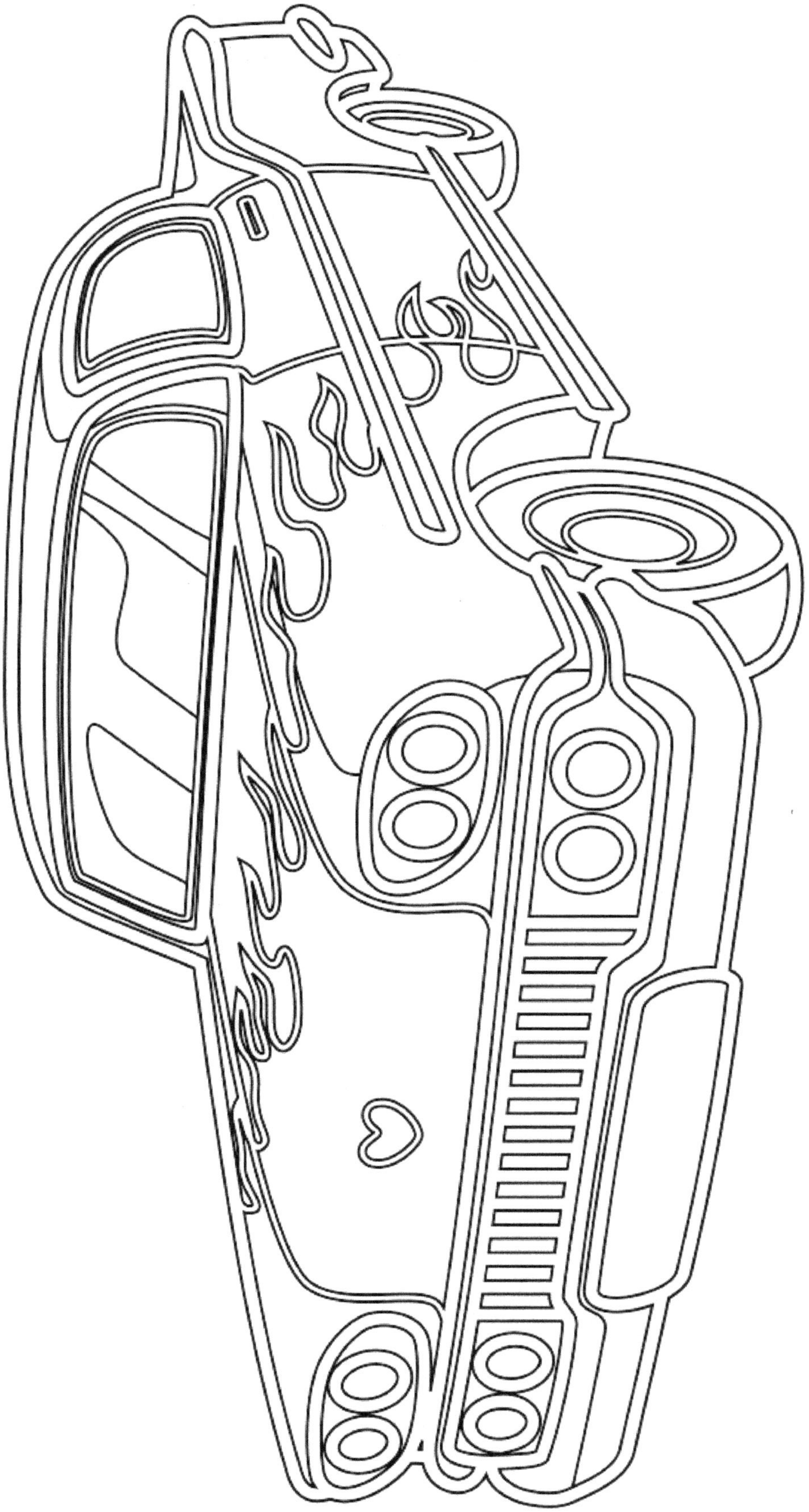

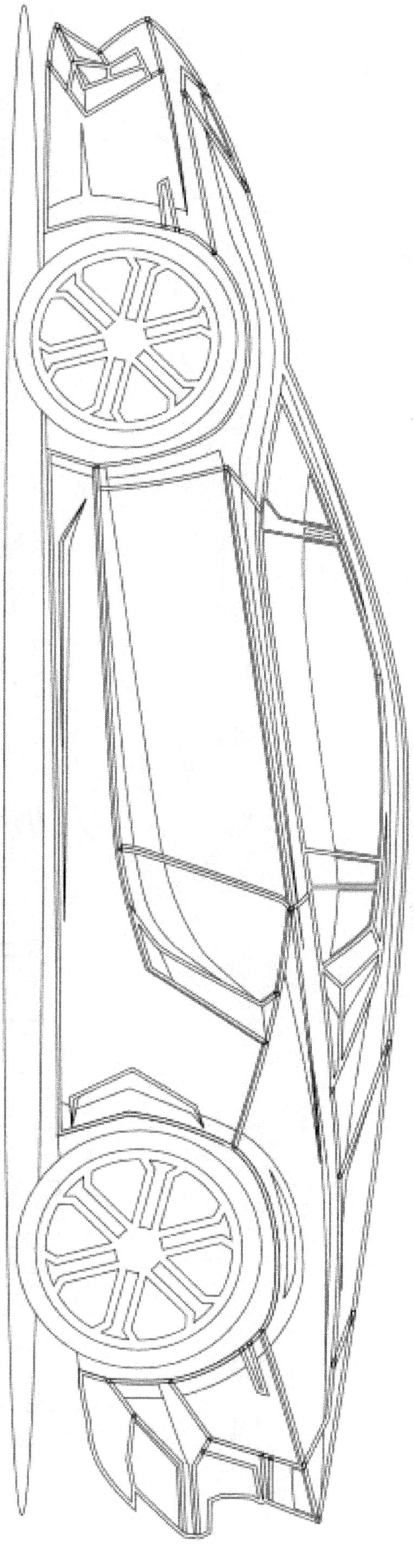

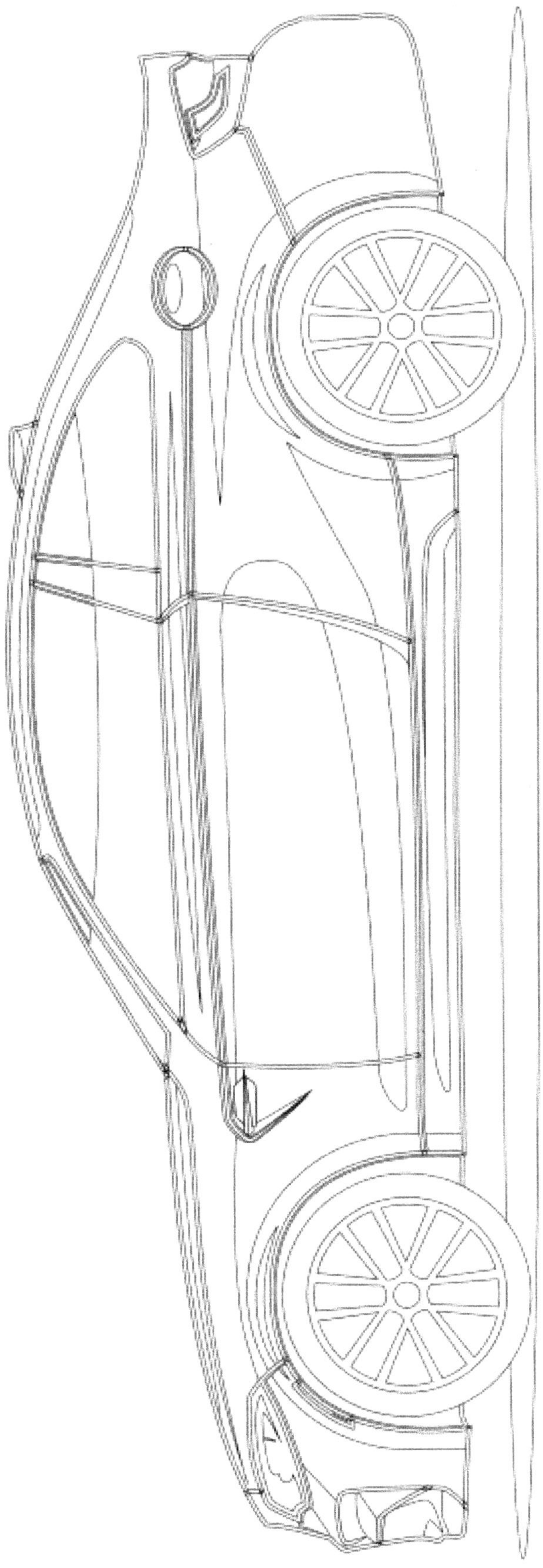

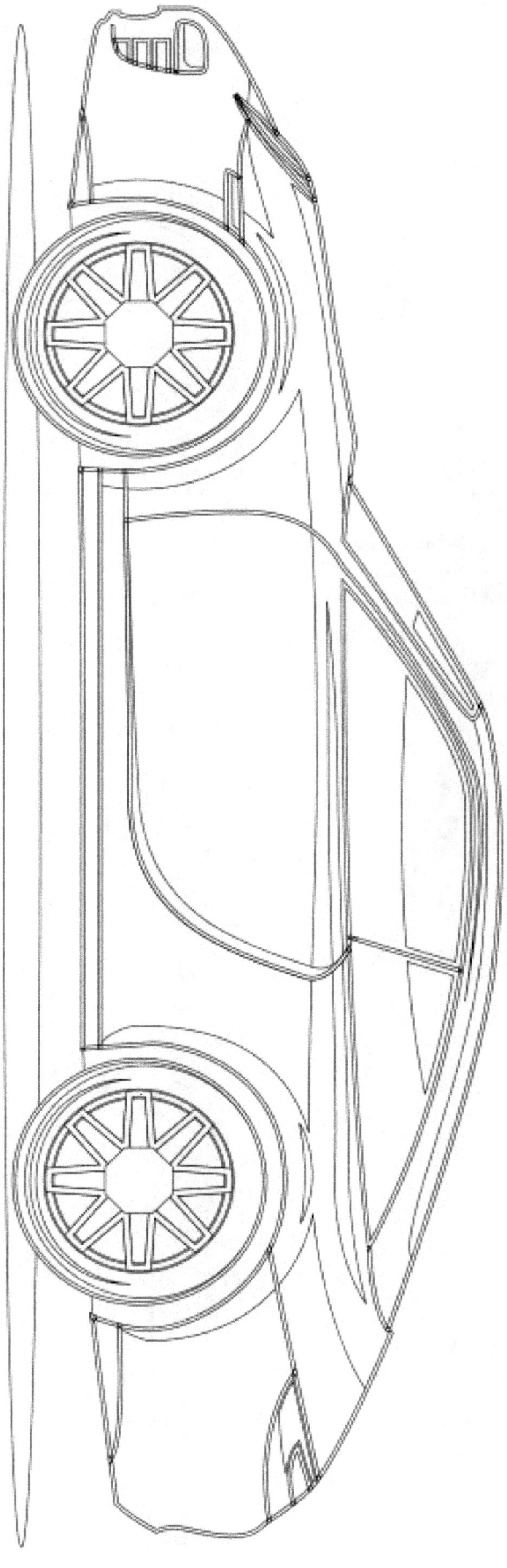

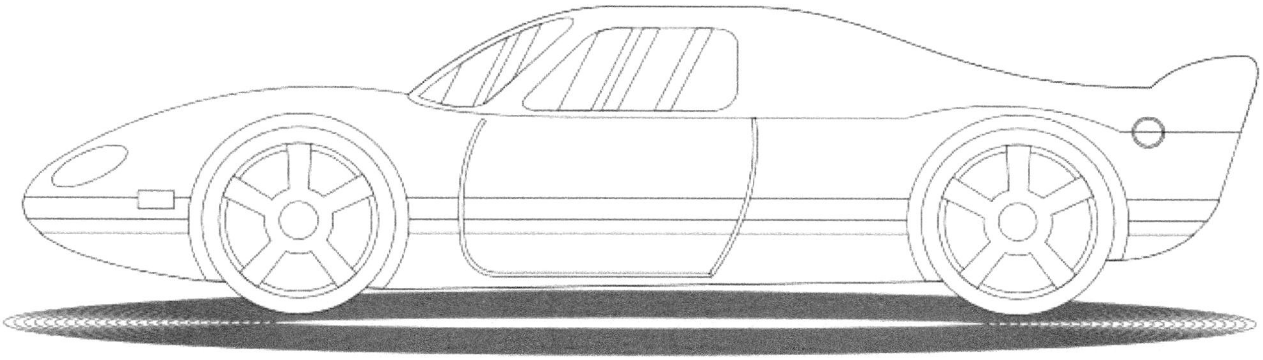

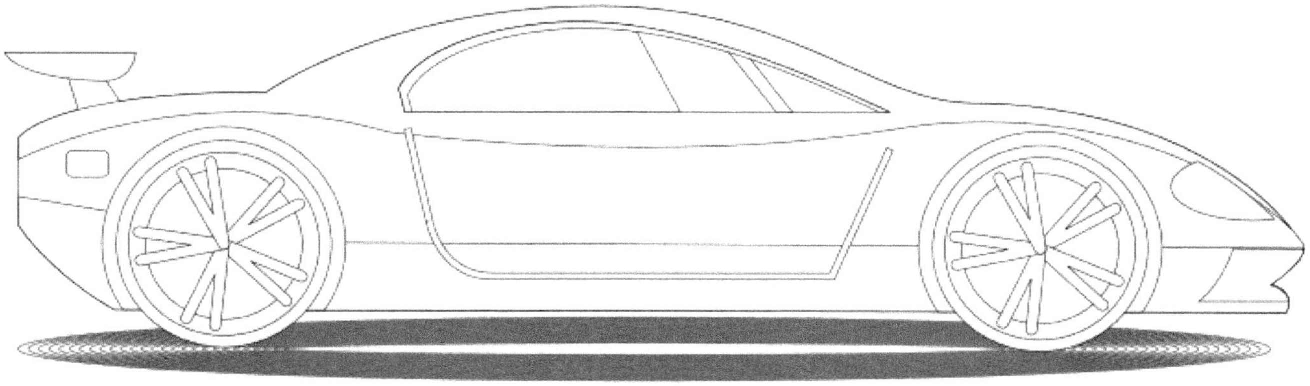

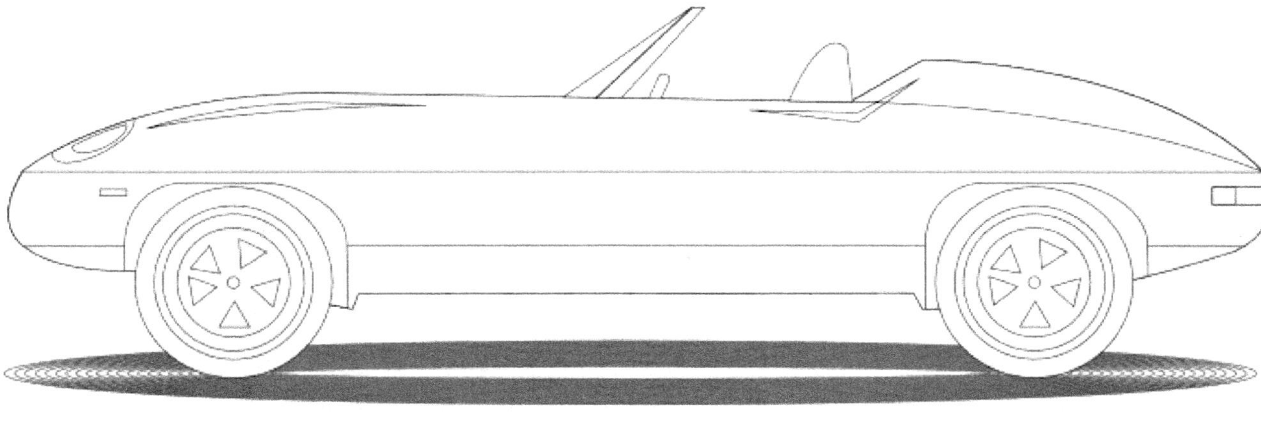

Printed in the USA
CPSIA information can be obtained
at www.ICGtesting.com
CBHW081152111224
18820CB00032B/449

9 798640 723847